W0081712

To Calvin Jay Miller,
stay cool

DE

For Meg and Grace,
friends since the Ice Age

ER

Text copyright © 2023 by David Elliott
Illustrations copyright © 2023 by Ellen Rooney

All rights reserved. No part of this book may be reproduced,
transmitted, or stored in an information retrieval system
in any form or by any means, graphic, electronic, or
mechanical, including photocopying, taping, and recording,
without prior written permission from the publisher.

First edition 2023

Library of Congress Catalog Card Number 2022922952
ISBN 978-1-5362-0599-2

APS 28 27 26 25 24 23
10 9 8 7 6 5 4 3 2 1

Printed in Humen, Dongguan, China

This book was typeset in Columbus MT.
The illustrations were created using printmaking ink, gouache,
crayon, and digital and traditional collage techniques.

Candlewick Press
99 Dover Street
Somerville, Massachusetts 02144

www.candlewick.com

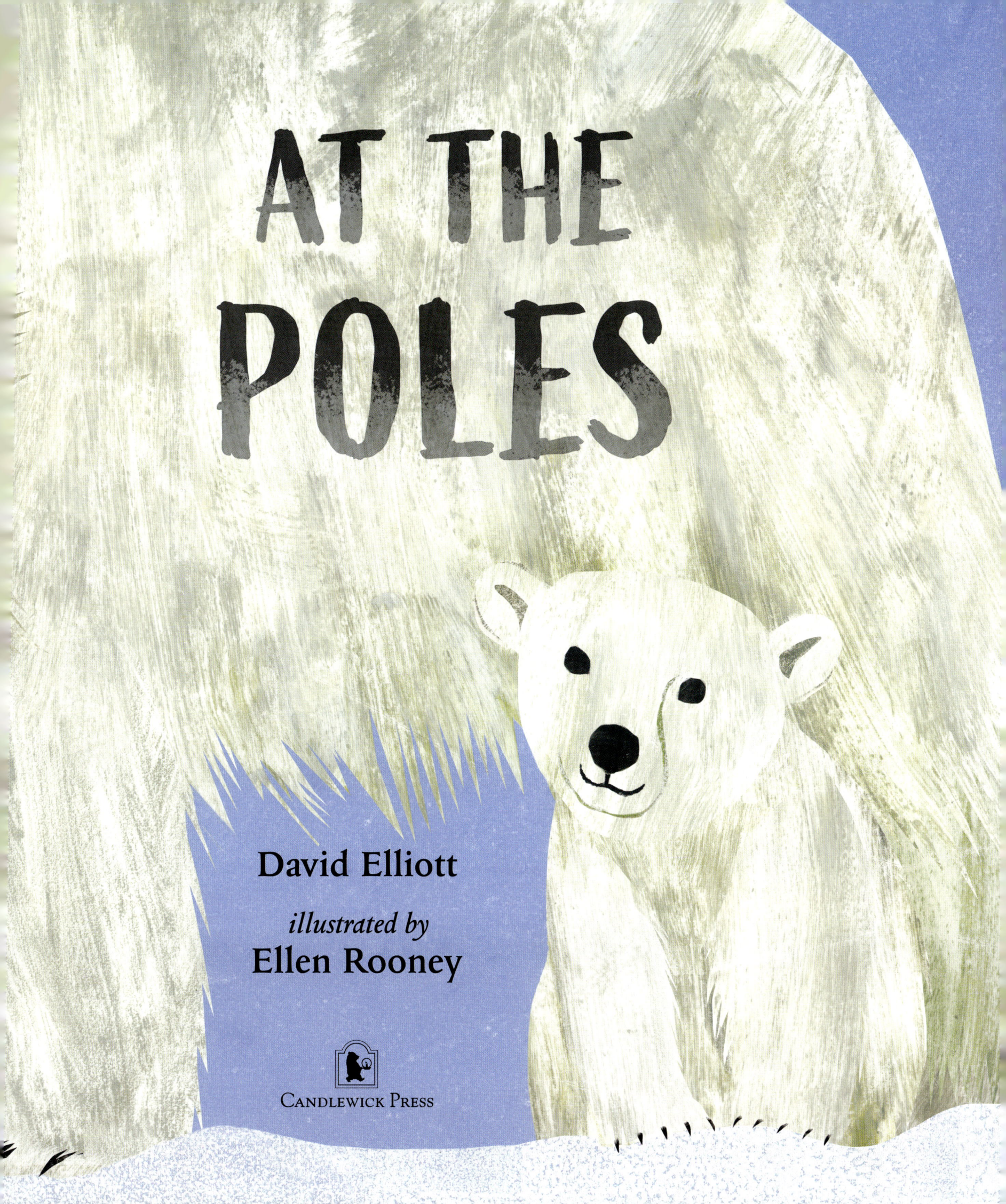

AT THE POLES

David Elliott

illustrated by
Ellen Rooney

CANDLEWICK PRESS

Antarctic

EMPEROR PENGUIN

All Hail the Monarch
of a Vast and Frozen Nation!

Cheers to the Master
of Parental Dedication!

Praise for the Ruler
of Long-Distance Ambulation!

Long Live the Emperor
of Close Cooperation!

ANTARCTIC KRILL

Small but monumental,
the krill is fundamental
to the Southern Ocean

and a tribute

to the wonders
that the small
can set in motion.

SOUTHERN ELEPHANT SEAL

Your weight is second
only to the whale's.
It's impressive, the
way you tip the scales.

But how do you ex-
plain your tremendous
amplitude when you
sometimes go for months
without a single
bite of food?

COLOSSAL SQUID

The largest eyes of any beast?
The largest spineless thing that lives?

I must say,
to say the least,
you're a study in superlatives.

ANTARCTIC SHAG

The fish

at the

bottom

of the

Antarctic Ocean

are in a   sudden   panic,

fluttering   in constant   motion

like a sea   of silver

flags.

What could

be the   reason?

A raft of blue-eyed shags!

Arctic/Antarctic

ORCA

You have a reputation
        both
thrilling and widespread.

You inspire admiration,
        awe,
and not a little dread.

You employ echolocation,
        which
helps you keep well fed.

You are a master of predation
        from
the kingdom of the dead.

TARDIGRADE

You're almost indestructible.
You're nearly microscopic.
You prosper in Antarctic seas
and also in the tropics.

Some say you are *moss piglet*,
others *water bear*.
But no matter what we call you,
we find you everywhere.

Arctic

WALRUS

Small of eye and long of tusk,
aggressive, noisy, big and brusque,
the walrus is a *pinniped*.

(That means he has flippers.)

He's often in a social mood.
His whiskers help him find his food
and also ornament his head.

(The tusks are used as grippers.)

MUSK OX

The musk ox
is a paradox
because this ox
is *not* an ox.

Hooves
and horns
and shaggy coat.

He's closer to
a mountain goat.

NARWHAL

A singular creature
with a singular feature.

RIBBON SEAL

That banded pelt—so dashing!
How did you acquire it?
A shame you like the hermit's life;
there's no one to admire it.

GREENLAND SHARK

We say that wisdom
comes with age. If that
is true, Slow-Moving
One, then you must be
the weary sage
of the vast and
freezing Arctic seas.
You do not count
your life in years but
in the rippling
centuries.

CARIBOU

You lift your head
and velvet antlers rise
like a Viking chalice
lit by northern skies
and the aurora borealis.

ARCTIC HARE

Larger than your timid cousin
   the rabbit,
you have developed a fascinating
   habit.

A brilliant
   white when snow is on the ground,
but in spring,
   you change your wintry coat to brown.

It's really quite remarkable, this camouflaging
   guile.
And just as awe-inspiring? Your splendid sense
   of style.

POLAR BEAR

On the ice
or in the sea.

We would not
love the world
so much
without
your lonely
majesty.

NOTES ABOUT THE ANIMALS

Antarctic

EMPEROR PENGUIN
Both male and female emperor penguins take turns caring for their egg (just one each breeding season) and newly hatched chick. While one parent keeps guard, the other may walk as far as 50 miles (80 kilometers) to their feeding grounds in the sea. When Antarctic winds roar and the temperature starts dropping, emperors form a huddle. Once the penguins in the center are warm, they move to the outside, allowing everyone to take advantage of the heat generated in the middle. We can learn a great deal from the emperor penguin.

ANTARCTIC KRILL
An individual krill may be only a couple of inches long, but when they swarm in the Southern Ocean, the mass can be seen from outer space. Krill have the largest biomass of any animal on the planet. In other words, if you compared the combined weight of, say, all the elephants on Earth with the combined weight of all the krill, the latter would be the winner. Nearly all Antarctic animals—from Adélie penguins to blue whales and humpback whales—depend on krill for their food.

SOUTHERN ELEPHANT SEAL
Southern elephant seals are much larger than their northern cousins; males weigh six to seven times more than the largest land carnivores, polar bears. That huge proboscis that gives the elephant seal its name is used by males to produce deafening roars during the breeding season.

COLOSSAL SQUID
The colossal or Antarctic squid may well be one of the most mysterious animals in the ocean. Although two colossal squid tentacles were found in the stomach of a whale in 1925, it was not until 1981 that an entire specimen was retrieved. Many sperm whales are covered with scars that scientists believe to be caused by the hooks on colossal squids' tentacles. This is a creature that can literally grab your attention.

ANTARCTIC SHAG
Antarctic or blue-eyed shags are the only cormorants that live in the Antarctic. They are excellent divers and often feed together in large groups called rafts. Individuals in the raft help out the group by diving down and scaring up fish from the bottom. By the way, the name blue-eyed shag is misleading. That blue is actually a ring of skin circling the eye.

Arctic/Antarctic

ORCA
Orcas, or killer whales, live in all the world's oceans. Their name is derived from a Roman god of the underworld, Orcus, and means "from the kingdom of the dead." They are famous for their skill at hunting in packs. Each pod of orcas develops its own vocalizations and calls that are passed down from generation to generation, just as an accent or expression might be passed down in a human family.

TARDIGRADE
Tiny tardigrades, also known as water bears or moss piglets, are found all over the world and may well be the most adaptable animals living on Earth. They can manage temperatures as cold as -328˚F (-200˚C) and as hot as 300˚F (150˚C). They can even survive the radiation of outer space.

Arctic

WALRUS

The walrus's tusks, sometimes as long as 3 feet (1 meter), are not just for gripping the ice. They are great weapons, too, especially when a walrus must defend itself against an attacking polar bear or an orca, its only natural predators. A walrus can weigh as much as a Volkswagen Beetle. That's a lot of blubber.

MUSK OX

The musk ox is a great example of how it can be a mistake to judge a book by its cover: although musk oxen look as if they are members of the cattle family, they are more closely related to sheep and goats. Musk oxen have lived in the Arctic for thousands of years. Beneath their outer shaggy coat is a layer of extremely fine wool, called qiviut, which northern Indigenous people spin into a wonderfully soft yarn.

NARWHAL

In the Middle Ages, narwhals' spiraled ivory tusks were sold to European royalty as horns of the mythical unicorn. Hundreds of years later, that tusk remains a mystery; we still don't understand its purpose. What we do know is that it's actually a tooth that grows through the narwhal's upper lip. Ouch!

RIBBON SEAL

Unlike other seals, which live in herds, ribbon seals are solitary animals. They differ from other seals, too, in the way they move. Most seals get around on the ice by flexing their hind flippers and lifting their torso from the ground, kind of like the way a caterpillar moves. But ribbon seals make alternating strokes with their front flippers while they sway their hips from side to side.

GREENLAND SHARK

Greenland sharks have the longest life span of any vertebrate, or animal with a backbone, on Earth, living up to 250 years.

CARIBOU

Caribou and reindeer are the same species. The main difference between them is that most reindeer are domesticated while herds of caribou still run wild in the Arctic. Caribou are famous for their long migrations, nearly 600 miles (950 kilometers). Caribou are also the only animals in the deer family in which both males and females have antlers.

ARCTIC HARE

In addition to their size—hares are larger—there are other differences between hares and rabbits. When a rabbit senses danger, it freezes, whereas a hare uses its big hind feet to get out of there! An arctic hare's fur changes color depending on the season—except for the tips of its ears, which are always black.

POLAR BEAR

What can be said about the magnificent polar bear, the iconic animal of the Arctic? That it is the largest land carnivore on the planet? That underneath its fur, its skin is actually black? That for thousands of years it has played an indispensable role in the material and spiritual life of polar peoples? Whatever is said seems inadequate. The polar bear has become a symbol of the devastating effect climate change is having in the Arctic.